Also By JAMES MARSH STERNBERG

Playing to Trick One – No Mulligans in Bridge (2nd Ed)

Trump Suit Headaches; Rx for Declarers and Defenders

The Finesse; Only a Last Resort

Blocking and Unblocking

Shortness – a Key to Better Bidding (2nd Ed)

When Michaels Met The Unusual

From Zero to Three Hundred; A Bridge Journey

Reversing the Dummy

Trump Promotion; The Uppercut

Active or Passive – Becoming a Better Defender

The Redouble Mystery

I, Radiologist, The Evolution of Medicine in 'West' West Broward County

James Marsh Sternberg with Danny Kleinman

Second Hand High; Third Hand Not So High

An Entry, An Entry, My Kingdom For An Entry

L O L; Loser on Loser

In Search of a Second Suit

Elimination and Endplay

Suit Preference; Abused and Misused

I, RADIOLOGIST,

and The Evolution of Medicine in 'West' West Broward County, Florida

James Marsh Sternberg, MD

authorHOUSE®

AuthorHouse™
1663 Liberty Drive
Bloomington, IN 47403
www.authorhouse.com
Phone: 833-262-8899

Published by AuthorHouse 05/02/2023

ISBN: 979-8-8230-0744-3 (sc)
ISBN: 979-8-8230-0743-6 (e)

Print information available on the last page.

Any people depicted in stock imagery provided by Getty Images are models, and such images are being used for illustrative purposes only.
Certain stock imagery © Getty Images.

This book is printed on acid-free paper.

Because of the dynamic nature of the Internet, any web addresses or links contained in this book may have changed since publication and may no longer be valid. The views expressed in this work are solely those of the author and do not necessarily reflect the views of the publisher, and the publisher hereby disclaims any responsibility for them.

CONTENTS

DEDICATION

To

STEPHEN ALAN SCHULMAN, MD

(1936 – 2022)

My best friend, my partner
Thanks for the great ride

JMS

ACKNOWLEDGMENTS

I want to thank the late Dr. Nathanial 'Nate' Safran and the late Dr. Bernard 'Bernie' Epstein. Nate first piqued my interest in radiology and Bernie taught me what it means to be a radiologist.

Special thanks to Pearl Feiss for her editorial suggestions.

James Marsh Sternberg, MD
Palm Beach Gardens, FL

mmay001 @ aol.com

PRELUDE

This is a true story, a story of how medicine began in the far western part of Broward county. And of course, some of my own story because I was so intimately involved in the evolution of the development of medicine in that area. It mainly covers the period in west Broward from 1967 to 1988. There are also some chapters detailing the events leading up to and following these years.

But since I'm writing this tale in 2023 without notes, I'm sure a lot of both funny and sad stories are missing that would have been included had I known I was going to undertake this venture. Some of the photos are mine, some are from the internet, unfortunately some have been lost.

But I thought this story might be of some interest, especially to those of you who were there.

I hope so.

When I grow up, I want to be a radiologist

"Go West, Young Man, Go West". Everyone has heard this expression first used by John Babsone Lane Soule in the Terre Haute Express in 1851. It appealed to Horace Greeley, who rephrased it slightly in an editorial in the New York Tribune on July 13, 1865 as "Go West, young man, and grow up with the country."

Well, I did. And this book is my story. Was I lucky? Maybe. Was it out of desperation? Partly, for sure. Certainly I was in the right place at the right time. But in any case, I was one of the pioneers in the field of what became joint ventures, physician owned centers, self referral and all the subsequent legislation.

But I like to think I started medicine in the boondocks of 'west' west Broward. But west Broward now has become almost central Broward, from dirt roads to busy four-lane highways, from cow pastures to large shopping malls and huge population growth. Land that sold for $40,000 for twenty acres now sells for that price per foot of frontage property. Back when I was in medical school, had I been smart (and had some money), I probably should have bought all of south Florida.

If I hadn't started the first two hospitals out west in the middle of nowhere, sure, certainly someone else would have. There was nowhere else to go except west. I've included a few photos to try to give you a feel of what west Broward was like years ago, as well as a few personal photos.

And this is the story of how I as a young radiologist followed Horace Greeley's advice. I grew up with the county and it grew up with me.

Chapter One – Medical School Choices

As June approached, I was going to be graduating from Columbia College in New York City in June. My memories of the four years at college are very vague. While I could remember almost every teacher and most of my classmates from Nichols, a private high school in Buffalo, I could not recall any of my teachers from my college days. Most of my time was spent with my fraternity brothers at Zeta Beta Tau or with the golf team at Rockland County Golf Club across the Hudson River. My times in class were very vague. College life seemed easy. I was pre-med and even back then I knew I wanted to be a radiologist.

I had grown up in Buffalo, New York, the land of snow. I recall always either shoveling snow or taking people to see Niagara Falls. My father was a general practitioner and his best friend, Nathanial Safran, was a radiologist. I can remember spending many hours sitting in Nat's office while he was reading x-rays. This certainly was the major Influence on my decision to become a radiologist.

When it came time to apply to medical school, I had only a few choices. My grades were B+ and I had done little else at school to distinguish myself. Other than being captain of the golf team, for two years I was assistant manager of the varsity basketball team. Not a great resume. I applied to Upstate Medical Center in Syracuse, Downstate Medical Center in Brooklyn, Columbia Presbyterian in Manhattan, and the University of Miami in Florida. My parents had often taken us on vacation to Florida, usually to Palm Beach and we had loved the change of weather from the cold north. The University of Miami however, at that time was a state school really only for Floridians.

In late July, I received an acceptance from Syracuse, which was logical my being from upstate New York. I drove to Syracuse and made arrangements for living quarters. The same day, upon returning home to Buffalo, there was an envelope from the University of Miami. The University of Miami was going to accept four out-of-state applicants and for some unknown reason I was one. Did I want to attend?

Let's see. Syracuse and more snow or Miami with sunshine? This was not a hard choice. The last two years of college I had been dating a girl from Long Island. As graduation approached, her parents kept looking at me and I could see the question on their faces, "So when are you going to get married?"

I was pretty naïve when it came to girls. Nichols was an all-boys high school and Columbia had not yet gone co-ed. Barnard College for girls was only just across the street. I previously had hardly dated and certainly had not ever been in any other serious relationship, so...

Meanwhile the decision of which medical to choose school wasn't a difficult choice. Of course, it was Miami, here I come.

Jim and Barbara Are Married at the Waldorf

Chapter Two – Medical School, Internship

I got married at the Waldorf Astoria in Manhattan and drove off in my non-airconditioned Dodge Dart for Miami. In those days, the first two years of medical school were in Coral Gables next to what is now the Biltmore Hotel. In the late 50's and 60's, it was the VA Hospital.

I rented an apartment and bought an air-conditioned car. The first year of medical school was rather easy compared to the second year. The second year I needed to take some pills every day just to stay awake to study. But the Biltmore golf course was right next door to the medical school. I often snuck out of the afternoon labs to play nine holes.

The third and fourth years of medical school were at Jackson Memorial Hospital in Miami. I rented the downstairs of a duplex near the hospital. Now for the first time in my life, after having attended an all-boys high school and college, I was suddenly surrounded by women.

Nurses, nurses, and more nurses. And what was strange was they seemed more interested in the married medical students, interns, and residents than in the single guys. I don't know; maybe they were there to have a good time without commitments. There was a party every night in one of the nurses apartments. I didn't miss a single one.

I remember suggesting to a cousin who was single at the time and finishing medical school elsewhere that he do his internship at Jackson, thinking he would love it. He went and later told me he hated the experience. The nurses wanted nothing to do with him. Was it because he was single? That was his excuse. He never forgave me.

And where was I supposed to be those evenings? Why in the library studying of course. If someone called the library looking for a student, the librarian had the same stock answer. "Sorry, he's busy in the stacks studying, can I take a message?" I and everyone else went thru all those nurses like General Grant going thru Atlanta.

And it wasn't just evenings. I can recall sneaking out of a class to go sailing in Biscayne Bay with a nurse and we capsized the boat. I don't remember how I explained that one. By the end of my third year and the entire fourth year, I was going with only one nurse from New Jersey. Of course, by the time graduation rolled around, the relationship with my wife did not continue. I was lucky to be going to intern at Long Island Jewish Hospital in New Hyde Park, New York, considered a fine place for internship.

At Long Island Jewish Hospital, I immediately applied for the position of radiology resident for the following year and was accepted. In those days, radiology was not nearly as popular a specialty as it is today. I simply went to see Dr. Bernard Epstein, the chief of radiology and asked him for the position. He immediately said yes, likely because I was on the house staff and had priority, or more likely no one else had applied. There was only one resident position per year at that time.

I probably was a terrible intern. The rotation work schedule of 'on' 36 hours, then 'off' 12 hours left little free time for a social life. I did meet some local women and was dating one in particular.

I counted down the days till July 1, 1963. I hated every day of my internship. I couldn't even learn how to read an EKG properly. But I somehow survived. On June 30,1963 at the end of my shift, I put my intern whites and my stethoscope in a barrel and burned everything. The next day, July 1, I showed up in the radiology department dressed up, shirt, tie, and a jacket. I was now a radiologist!

Chapter Three – Residency

I took to radiology like a duck to water. I had been waiting my whole life for this and loved every minute of it. I breathed, ate, and slept being a radiologist. I learned everything I could. I never missed a moment or a chance to do a procedure. Dr. Epstein gave me one of his books and signed it "to one of my best residents!"

I was remarried (no Waldorf Astoria this time) by the local justice of the peace and lived in Great Neck. Life was good. I loved what I was doing. A close friend from medical school, Stephen Schulman, had switched from pediatrics to radiology partly at my urging. He had been a year ahead of me in school but was drafted into the navy after his first year of residency at Jackson. When he came out of the navy, he applied to Long Island Jewish. behind me.

Bernard S. Epstein, M.D.
1906–1978

Stephen and I owed Dr. Epstein a lot. We loved working under him; he was the greatest. But on the other hand, Dr. Epstein was a bit of a stickler. No one, and I mean no one ever 'ordered' an x-ray. If you said that to Dr. Epstein, he would say that if you wanted to order something, go to the cafeteria. If you needed a chest x-ray, you had to request a radiological consultation. "We are not a lab," he would say. I once saw him physically throw someone out of his office. But of course, he was right.

Send in a request form, write down the problem and what you were looking for, and the radiologist would do the 'ordering.' You don't send a patient to a surgeon and tell him what kind of surgery to do, what incision to make, what sutures to use, do you? To this day, when I hear someone say "order an x-ray of_____", I get chest pain. Even just the word 'order' still affects me.

This of course became deeply ingrained within me and would come back to haunt me in my career. More on that later. But he was correct.

What a difference between being an intern, doing everything no one wanted to do, and being a radiology resident with Dr. Epstein. Since in those days, computerized tomography had not yet come into medical use, taking weekend and night call was easy. The emergency physician rarely called me. Today in most teaching hospitals there is usually a radiology resident in the hospital 24/7.

Dr. Epstein was the nicest guy, but others in the hospital were a bit nervous around him. I recall taking call on the golf course with my beeper one Sunday afternoon and Dr. Phillip Lear, the Chief of Surgery called me, right while I was putting. Some nerve! He had a patient with a suspected kidney stone and wanted me to come in and do a series of x-rays to confirm his diagnosis. Remember, this was a department chief talking to a first-year resident.

I knew the radiology department policy was we did not do this examination routinely on weekends unless the patient was going to surgery the same day. I timidly asked, "Dr. Lear, are you planning to operate today if we find a kidney stone?" After a bit of silence, Dr. Lear said "No." So I said, "OK, let me run this by Dr. Epstein to get approval and then I'll be glad to come in." After another bit of silence, I hear "Maybe I'll give him a morphine drip and we can do it tomorrow."

One afternoon I was reading films and the phone rang. I answered and it was a friend of mine, one of the internists on staff. He asked me if I would find the x-ray report for him on one of his patients. "Sure," I said. Just then Dr. Epstein walked in the room and asked, "Jim, who is on the phone?" When I told him, he grabbed the phone and said "Get one of your medical residents to find the report. My residents are busy!" and hung up!

Yes, Bernie always had our backs. Once I presented films at a medical conference and really screwed it up. Afterwards, the Chief of Medicine came to Dr. Epstein's office and said something to the effect of "Your resident said 'black is white'," or something to that effect. Bernie said "of course black is white" and threw him out. Later he called me in his office privately and asked me, "Jim, you idiot. Why did you tell them 'black was white'?"

After completing my three-year residency (today a radiology residency is four years), Stephen and I were board eligible and went to Pittsburgh to take our board examinations. Stephen was eligible the same year as I since his two-year stint as a radiologist in the navy counted for one year. The board exams in those days were oral and actually quite easy. It was the fear leading up to them that was scary.

Having completed my residency, I wasn't sure what to do nex . I was offered a position to stay on at Long Island Jewish as an attending radiologist which I accepted. First question I had was, do I now call Dr. Epstein 'Bernie' as all the other doctors did? I had always been on a first name basis with all the attending physicians ever since my first year as a resident. But somehow I couldn't get the word 'Bernie' out of my mouth.

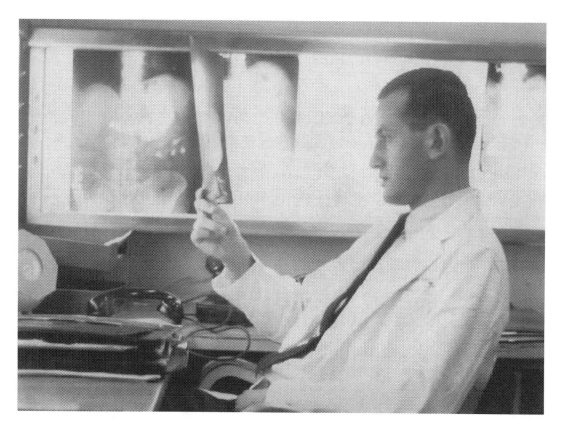

I'm finally a radiology resident

Jim and Lorraine 1966

Chapter Four – Florida License

When a medical student graduated from the University of Miami School of Medicine, he or she automatically received a Florida license to practice medicine and surgery. In the 1960's and 70's, it was very difficult to get a Florida license. Many northern physicians wanted to semi-retire to Florida. But there was no state reciprocity and it was almost impossible to pass the exam; the 'results' were predetermined.

If you were from out-of-state, you were destined to flunk the test. I don't think they even bothered to grade the exam. They just looked to see where you were from. All Floridians passed, everyone else failed. There were lots of tales about how much money it took to 'buy' a license. On the other hand after graduation from Miami with a license, one did not need any post-graduate training. Take that license, head up to north Florida and open an office for business the next day. Scary.

One day after about six months working as an attending radiologist, I received a long distance phone call from a complete stranger. The conversation went something like this:

Me: "Hello?"

Caller: "Is this Dr. James Sternberg?"

Me: "Yes, what can I do for you? Who is this?"

Caller: "My name is Dr. Andre Capi. Is it true you have a Florida medical license?"

Me: "Yes, I do."

Caller: "How would you like a nice job in the Ft Lauderdale area?"

Me: Silence

Caller: "Hello, are you still there?"

Me: "Yes, can you tell me a little more?"

Caller: "How about if we fly you down for a few days to see if our practice might be something you would like?"

Myself, Lorraine, Cheryl and Andre Capi
MY FIRST BOSS. WE WERE LOVING BEING IN S. FLORIDA

Game, set, match. I looked at the snow outside. The next thing I knew, we were on a plane to south Florida. We had dinner with Andre and Cheryl Capi in their beautiful waterfront home in Pompano Beach.

Andre was the head of a three-man practice, Capi, Avellone, and Klein, with Klein doing the radiotherapy. Andre Capi and Ted Avellone covered two private offices and three small hospitals and were looking for another diagnostic radiologist. They were paying considerably more than I was making at Long Island Jewish. I was hooked!

I thought about the four years I had been in Florida during medical school and the many times I had visited Palm Beach on vacation with my parents. How could we not go? Going north for my post graduate training was a wise decision, but it was cold. Those memories of winters in Buffalo still lingered deep within.

What was there to even think about? Pack the bags!!

Ft Laud Beach circa 1965 – 1970. A nice quiet town along the ocean. Emphasis on the word quiet after moving from New York.

Ft Lauderdale - Hollywood International Airport circa 1970
A feel of what Broward county was like back in the 1960 – 1970 era.

Chapter Five – One Year in Hollywood

So in early 1967, I moved to Hollywood Florida and rented a small house. Now I was in private practice, a big shot in a small community. Our group covered two small hospitals, Golden Isles Hospital in Hallandale and Doctor's Hospital in east Hollywood. We had private offices in Hollywood and Pompano Beach so a lot of time was spent in the car driving from place to place.

At first it was very exciting. I was or thought I was getting along fine with all the referring physicians. Most of them knew little about radiology and I felt very comfortable. The only drawback to the job was the driving. At that time, I-95 extended north only as far as the center of Ft Lauderdale, around the level of Alligator Alley. In those days, the Alley was a two-lane road to Naples.

What I was unaware of at the time was my attitude. Having spent almost four years working with Dr. Epstein, I had inherited a lot of his attitude. But there was a big difference between working in a hospital as a radiologist where the department ran as the chief wanted, and working in private practice. In the latter, volume and keeping the referring physicians happy were the key to a successful practice.

Well, I'm sure you can guess the rest of the story. As I neared the end of my first year, Capi, Avellone, and Klein informed me my services would no longer be needed. I guess I had pissed off too many of their referring physicians with my attitude. Looking back on it, I'm sure they were probably right. And meanwhile, I had just bought a big new house for $75.000, a fortune in those days. Great, big new mortgage, no job.

Thanks, Bernie.

Chapter Six – Out of Work; Office?

So now what? Jobs were scarce in south Florida. After all, where would you want to go if you were looking for a job, south Florida or the Dakotas? I searched unsuccessfully for a new position for a couple of months. I did work for a few months on a temporary basis at the Miami Heart Institute, but the driving distance was too much.

Finally, I found two part-time positions. Dr. Curt Meltzer at Parkway General Hospital in North Miami Beach was looking for a part-time radiologist and Dr. Robert Liebeskind at Plantation General Hospital, which had opened in 1966, was also looking for a part-time radiologist.

I had known Bob at Jackson when he was a radiology resident and I was a fourth-year medical student. We worked out a schedule where I worked at both hospitals on a part-time basis. Curt had nothing more to offer future wise. However, Bob, who had been working alone at Plantation was expecting to be drafted. He told me that if I could cover the hospital until he returned, we would become equal partners.

Plantation was a rural town, the most western part of Ft Lauderdale and had been there forever. The western boundary was University Drive, but in fact there wasn't much west of Route 441 where Plantation General was located. The only thing west was a two-lane dirt road, and land, with cow pastures everywhere.

This arrangement of back and forth between Plantation and north Miami had been satisfactory at the time. I expected to switch to Plantation General full time when Bob was drafted. Things were looking up. It seemed I had even learned how to get along with the referring physicians despite still cringing every time I heard the word 'order'.

Of course, nothing ever works out as planned. Somehow, Bob got exempted from the draft. As soon as he was sure he was exempt, he told me he no longer needed my services. He said that none of the referring physicians liked me, and he was letting me go. What a crock.

But during the months I was at Plantation, I felt I had developed a good rapport with most of the referring physicians. In the medical plaza right in front of Plantation General was a small private radiology office owned and operated by Dr. Jack Purcell. Jack had two offices, one on the east side of town near Holy Cross Hospital and this smaller office.

The great majority of Jack's time was spent in his east office. The west office had one x-ray table. It didn't have an automatic processor, but could do basic work. Jack was grossing a pittance in this office, mostly because so often he was not there when needed. I had a few meetings with Jack and he was amenable to the idea of selling the office to me.

Contrary to what Bob had told me, I felt I had developed a good rapport with many of the Plantation physicians despite my short time in town. I had already learned my lesson the hard way. I spoke to many of the local physicians and told them I was considering buying Jack's office. Would they send their out-patient work to me instead of to Bob next door at the hospital? The responses were very favorable since I would be available full time.

So OK, screw you Bob. I bought the office and opened for business early in August 1968. One machine, one technician, and one secretary. Bring 'em on!

Chapter Seven – Love My Office

I was certainly a little fish but in a little pond. However, through my past mistakes, I had discovered the key to success – service. My referring doctors knew I was always available. They knew I was in the office and they would get a report right away. This was not important for patients who had examinations scheduled. But for patients with trauma, or cough, problems that needed an answer right away, I was there. I called every report to the referring physician. It was a small community and when I had time (I wasn't exactly swamped with work at the beginning), I either walked or drove over and showed the film to the referring physician. They were very impressed. No one had ever done that before.

This was also a period of growth of the number of physicians opening practices in the Planation area. The great majority were displaced Cuban physicians. In the late 1960's, there was a great influx of physicians leaving Cuba for Florida. And where could they practice? Miami was well staffed as was east Broward. At least 50% of my referring physicians were Cuban and so were the patients. My Spanish was pretty good, at least good enough. Eventually, they even made me an honorary member of the local Cuban Medical Society.

I worked mainly in the dark room. My technician took the films, but I was in the dark room, hand developing the films, reloading the film cassettes, and calling the referring physician from the dark room. They would tell me to either send the patient back to their office, tell the patient everything was OK, or to go home and the doctor would call them. I always tried to personally meet and introduce myself to every patient. It was very unusual for a radiologist, and certainly unheard of today.

What do patients complain about the most? Do you know what that is? What do you hate when you have an appointment? Yes, waiting, sometimes it seems forever. No patient ever waited in my practice. If you had a 10:00 AM appointment, you were called in at 10:00. I had four dressing rooms. Since I also had a lot of walk-in patients (I never turned anyone away), sometimes things got a bit crazy.

But if a patient had an examination scheduled at 10:00, into the dressing room at 10:00 they went. If they had a complicated examination, I often took one film, then put the patient back in the dressing room while I did the walk-in patients. Everybody was happy.

I learned to be a pretty good radiological technician. With only one technician there were days there was no technician. It was me or no one and I wasn't cancelling anyone or sending them elsewhere. I couldn't afford it. I even did some cases when my only machine was broken, and I was waiting for the General Electric repair man.

For example, for a barium enema, patients needed to take laxatives the night before. I put them on the table, made some noise pretending to take a film, then told them the film showed they were not adequately cleaned out. They would need to take another laxative and come back tomorrow. In the days before ultrasound, gall bladders were examined by taking pills the night before, then films taken the next morning. But it wasn't unusual to need another day, especially with a bad gall bladder. So again, lie down, noise, come back tomorrow. Finally, the GE repair man showed up and I was back in business.

The office grew rapidly. Patients were happy since they never waited and they met the radiologist. Referring physicians were happy since they knew I was always there so they could get an immediate report. And they could always send a patient without an appointment.

If a physician's office ever called and asked, "Do you have time to do such and such exam today?" the answer was always the same. How soon can he/she get here? I later added a second x-ray machine, table, and an automatic film processor. I started doing some nuclear medicine exams with a Picker rectilinear scanner, now a relic from the days of the dinosaurs. I no longer cared who 'ordered' what. Sorry, Bernie.

Some of the office patients were strange. I recall one patient came for a stomach examination, called a gastrointestinal (GI) study. In the office at that time this was one of the more expensive examinations, about $100 or so. (A pittance by today's standards). After an extensive study, I found the examination was normal and the referring physician told me to give the patient the good news. "Mr. X," I said. "Good news, your examination is normal." Was he happy? "You mean I spent $100 for nothing," he replied. "OK," I said. "You have terminal stomach cancer. Do you feel better now?"

Another patient, an attorney, came for a kidney exam. Before we started, while lying on the table he asked me how much this was going to cost. "About $100," I replied. He became belligerent (as most attorneys do) so I said "Let's do this on a contingency basis. If I find nothing wrong, there will be no charge. But if I find something wrong, I want one-third of ..." something or other, I don't exactly remember.

He got up, got dressed, and left. Now I understood why my dentist, a close friend for many years, had a standing policy in his dental office: no kids, no lawyers, and he stuck to it. He later told me it was the best decision he had ever made.

It was also a wise decision to follow Dr. Purcell's policy of not opening the office on Saturdays. Few of the doctors were working on Saturdays. But since half my referring physicians took Wednesdays off and half took Thursdays, I could not take a day off during the week.

But I was never happier. I was my own boss. My practice was thriving, I was quickly fitting in as a member of the local medical community.

Every December I had a big party at our house for all my referring physicians and their wives. I knew everyone. Compare this to the radiologist of the 2020's who probably has never met one of his referring physicians. Could things be any better?

Chapter Eight – What's Missing?

The answer to the question at the end of the previous chapter was yes and no. It was 1971 and while life at the office was all smiles, life at home was not. I was happier in the office than at home. Why? What went wrong with my second marriage? My wife was bored, but we had a full time housekeeper to help with the children. Me? Probably too much interest in work and maybe some secretaries, technicians, etc.

We bought a bigger house in Hollywood, tennis court and all. I kept commuting to my office in Plantation which was a bit of a ride. Remember, I-95 still only went half-way up to Plantation.

What was missing from my life? I found I missed the action of hospital radiology. The problem with a private office was most of the cases were normal. There wasn't any of the intellectual stimulus I had experienced as a hospital-based radiologist, with conferences, complicated cases and a more challenging workplace. Only rarely was there a case that was 'interesting' from a radiological point of view, and then that patient usually ended up in a hospital, lost to follow-up.

Chapter Nine – An Idea Forms

It seemed the only way I was going to add some hospital work to my life was to add some hours working for someone in a hospital. And having already been fired a couple of times, going back to working for someone did not seem like a workable option. Finally it dawned on me. The answer was to build my own hospital, unheard of in those days. Corporations like Extendicare (now Humana), Hospital Corporation of America, owned the hospitals.

Fortunately in those days, one did not need a Certificate of Need to build and open a hospital. This later did become a requirement to open a new facility. But where? Well, knowing that south Florida was bound to grow, there was only one direction. East? No, that would be in the Atlantic Ocean. North or South? Already built up and done. West? Yes!

In the early 1970's, the idea of physician owned facilities didn't exist. Heresy! Doctors making money from where they sent their patients? Unheard of. So I started the idea of physician partnerships owning medical facilities.

Remember, west Plantation was nothing but barren land, except for the cows, and the roads were dirt. But I knew that was going to change. It was inevitable; there was nowhere else to go for expansion, and besides, what other choice did I have.

Certainly if there was a new hospital way out there in the boondocks, it was only natural physician offices would follow, commercial ventures would follow, and new communities would start up.

A typical street in booming west Plantation
early 1960's
You can still get a lot now to build on if you hurry.

West Broward Blvd Plantation – *The main road in existing Plantation. It hadn't changed much by the time Plantation General Hospital was built in 1966, and that was even further west of this photo.*

Imagine what it looked like even further west where I was going.

Chapter Ten – West Broward Investments

I felt if I could convince enough doctors we needed another hospital, I could do this. I approached my good friend, Herbert Moselle, an ear, nose, and throat physician in my office complex with the idea. I convinced him that if we could get enough physicians interested, we could proceed. We formed West Broward Investments, LLC.

We had a feasibility study done and I began to talk to the local physicians. Herb and I felt if we could get fifteen to twenty physicians involved, we could get this venture going. I began making the rounds to talk to doctors and sell shares. Herb and I would be the general partners. The referring physicians would be limited partners with essentially no risk other than their initial investment. How much do you think that was?

The whooping sum of seven hundred dollars. Wow, you would have thought we were asking for their life savings and first-born child. At first, all I heard was "this is too much money, Plantation General will get mad at us and take away our admitting privileges, this is unethical," excuses, excuses, excuses. But fifteen doctors signed up to join. Now came the how and where?

I had a good friendship with George and Lynn Cravero. George was a general contractor who had built a number of buildings in Plantation, mainly office buildings. Herb and I approached George with this idea. He loved it at once. Now we had our 'how', the question was where?

Chapter Eleven – Max

Cravero had plans drawn up for a 250 bed hospital which he would build. That was fine, about a five million dollar project, a lot of money in those days. There was only one catch. George had built a lot of buildings, but never with a mortgage. We couldn't get financing. We needed someone with deep pockets and a credit line to cover the project.

Enter stage left- Max. Dr. Maxwell Dauer, PhD, was the medical physicist for the Department of Radiology at the University of Miami. Somehow, he had heard of our plans and liked the idea. He called me and we set up a meeting. Max wanted in. He said he had a couple of friends with big bucks and could probably provide or at least sign for the financing. Max wanted to join Herb and I as a general partner. At that time we didn't have many options. Herb and I scheduled a meeting in Tampa with Max's two other investors. We flew to Tampa in a four passenger private plane Max had rented.

The meeting went well and they were interested. There seemed to be no serious obstacles and we flew back. I still remember that flight, one that among other factors swore me off small planes. I had no clue about flying, but I was up front in the co-pilot seat with Herb and Max in the back. It was scary.

The pilot, an older man was at the controls, but he obviously had the shakes. Both hands trembled as he held the controls. As we flew he kept squinting at the panels, looking for I don't know what. Half-way home he turned to me and asked, "Can you read what the panels say?" Somehow, we made it back home but that was to be my last flight in a small aircraft.

I thought things were progressing well until Max told us a few more details. It seemed Max and Mrs Max owned a parcel of land of some thirty or so acres on West Oakland Park out west near the Florida Turnpike. Max's contribution was to be the land and there was one other caveat.

His son was in medical school and was going to be a radiologist. He would be finishing his residency in 1978 and who do you think Max was going to insist be Chief of Radiology? Yes, 'Max Jr' of course. That was the end of any further dealings with Max.

To his credit, a few years later, Max did build a hospital on that piece of land which was very successful, the Florida Medical Center.

Max died in November, 1990 choking to death in a restaurant after an unsuccessful Heimlich maneuver.

Chapter Twelve – Extendicare, Inc

If you drove west on West Broward Boulevard, west of what would become University Drive, there was nothing but empty space and cows. But on the southwest corner, for some years there had been a billboard advertising a coming shopping mall. A possible site?

Enter Extendicare, Inc, now known as Humana, Inc, a hospital company based in Louisville, Kentucky. After many hours on the phone, Humana was interested and agreed to a meeting in Plantation with our physician investor group. The president and board chairman of Extendicare were Wendall Cherry and David Jones. They agreed to meet with us in Cravero's office.

Great! A 7:30 PM meeting was scheduled and most of my group showed up. 7:30, no Humana. 7:45, no Humana. At 8:00, I went outside to look around the parking lot. I saw a man, 40 or so years old, wearing tattered jeans, an old shirt and sneakers wandering around. I ignored him until I heard "Jim, is that you?" Nobody could accuse Wendell of overdressing for this meeting. He just couldn't find the office.

At that time, Humana owned all their hospitals. But we wanted to own the hospital; we just wanted Humana to sign the necessary paperwork to pay for it. However, Wendall liked our idea, saw the future in it and said he would discuss the project with his board.

We came to an agreement. Humana would take care of the financing. They would have a five year management agreement with an option to purchase after the five years. We had a deal and were on our way! Lynwood Hospital, named after George's wife was ready to go.

So across the street on the north side of the proposed mall, we purchased a square shaped twenty acres. Ten acres in the back would be for the hospital, ten acres in the front for an office building and small stores.

We paid something like $40,000 for the whole package, which today probably sells for $40,000 per foot of frontage.

Future Broward Mall
View of the land across the street from the hospital where a sign
'Site of Broward Mall' had been posted for a few years.
The Mall was finally built and opened in
1978. For now, just the cows.

Our hospital was built right across the street of this
thriving community after we moved some cows.

University Drive in the beginning.

**About the time we were building the hospital.
This is now a busy six-lane highway in the center of town.**

Chapter Thirteen – Margate General

Meanwhile, remember the saying it never rains, it pours? At the time this was going on, Cravero had also purchased a two-story building in Margate, Florida. Margate was also way west, north of Plantation, a bit more developed than west Plantation but not by much. His plan was to turn it into a nursing home. But now Cravero had the hospital bug. It was a simple matter of changing the plans to a 150 bed hospital.

I worked with Cravero in making the changes, organized a medical staff, and appointed myself Chief of Radiology, with no contract, an important consideration that will be discussed in a later chapter. There were a sufficient number of physicians in the area to keep the beds mostly full and an emergency room. Cravero made a management deal with Hospital Corporation of America and we were open in 1972.

My plate was too full. I had to cover Margate General and the Plantation office. I hired a couple of radiologists, but I wasn't really satisfied with any to consider a long term arrangement. And in the meantime, we had pushed the cows out of the way and had a ground breaking ceremony for Lynwood Hospital. Construction was underway.

Initially we had a very good relationship with the Louisville company. While construction in Plantation was underway, Humana invited myself, Moselle and a busy endocrinologist in the area, Alberto Fernandez to Louisville for the 75th running of the Kentucky Derby.

That was a really fun weekend. After all, Humana was a big deal in Louisville so we went to many wonderful private parties and had special seats for the Derby. Some of the parties reminded me of Gone with the Wind, big mansions on huge acres, fancy balls, very nice. Everything looked great, too good to be true.

Margate

Aerial view circa 1970 – lots of empty space but a little more developed than the Plantation site

There were not many physician offices anywhere nearby, but that quickly changed once we opened Margate General Hospital.

The Center of Margate

A busy street in Margate circa 1970, but one could usually find a parking place.

The Busy Margate Mall – Circa 1970.
The hospital was built just down the street.

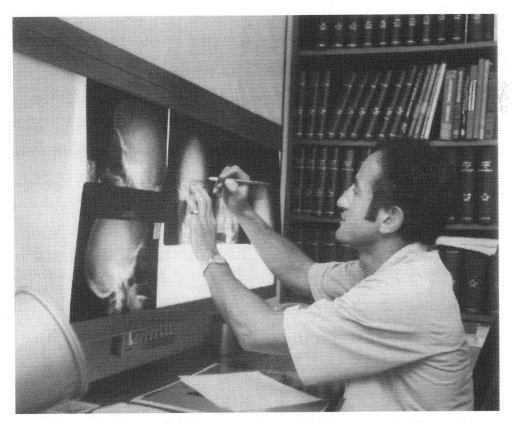

I'm back working at Margate General

Chapter Fourteen – Grant Bennett, MD

Finally I found a radiologist to work with me that I liked. Grant Bennett, from New York moved to Plantation. Our understanding was after one year, assuming all went well, it would be Sternberg and Bennett, PA. He was a very likeable guy, a good radiologist, and of course most important seemed to be developing a good working rapport with my referring physicians. I wanted a partner who was a competent radiologist with the right personality, rather than a genius who couldn't get along with the referring doctors. That had been me, but I had learned my lesson and now all the doctors loved me.

Grant had a wife, Cheryl, and a son of about six months. He also loved to fly and owned a small one-engine plane. He kept it in a hangar at Ft Lauderdale airport and spent lots of his free time in the air. We worked well together and were looking forward to the opening of Lynwood Hospital probably in late 1974. We knew we would likely hire additional radiologists and then make a decision about the office. Would it be profitable to keep it open if we were managing two hospitals? Maybe not, as much as I loved that office.

Everything was going too well. Grant took his family for a weekend vacation. I received a phone call at 3:00 AM. Grant's plane had crashed in the Carolinas killing himself, his wife and child. Everyone was devastated. What happened? Who knew? His parents in New York had been notified and the funerals would be in New York. Lots of questions, not many answers. It was very sad.

To digress, perhaps it was a foreboding. Over the next fifteen years of my career, six, yes six of my physician friends killed themselves piloting their own small aircraft. One was even an experienced stunt pilot. Each time such an accident occurred, another physician 'pilot' would be in my office explaining to me what the guy had likely done wrong.

Then bam! A few months later the same guy goes down. Like I mentioned in an early chapter, after my flight to Tampa with Max, I never flew again in a small plane, especially one flown by an amateur pilot like a cocky 'know-it-all' physician.

Another condition with a higher than normal incidence in physicians than the general population is suicide. During the course of my days as an active radiologist in west Broward, six of my physician friends fell victim to this terrible tragedy. There were a lot of sad days.

WEST BROWARD INVESTMENT LTD.

JAMES STERNBERG — HERBERT MOSELLE, General Partners

And

EXTENDICARE, INC., LOUISVILLE, KENTUCKY

WENDELL CHERRY, President

ANNOUNCE THAT LYNWOOD HOSPITAL

8200 WEST BROWARD BLVD., FT. LAUDERDALE, FLORIDA

HAS BEEN RENAMED AND WILL OPEN IN THE FALL OF 1974 AS

GRANT BENNETT COMMUNITY HOSPITAL

Chapter Fifteen – Stephen Schulman, MD

There was a lot to do. First, a mutual decision was made to change the name of the coming Plantation hospital to Grant Bennett Community Hospital. A subsequent office building behind the hospital later did became Bennett Plaza. And I needed a radiologist. Fortunately, I had someone in mind.

Remember Stephen Schulman from Chapter Three, my friend from medical school who was a resident with me and had gone into the navy. He had been stationed at Quonset Point, Rhode Island. We had remained close. I had visited him several times while he was in the navy. After his residency he had returned to Rhode Island to the Miriam Hospital in Providence. He had made many friends in the area while in the navy and felt comfortable staying in Rhode Island.

But Stephen was a Floridian at heart. He had gone to Miami High School, then college at Emory, then medical school in Miami. He completed one year of a pediatric residency at Jackson Memorial Hospital in Miami. He always wanted to be a pediatrician. I knew his parents well. They lived in south Miami and I was a frequent guest for dinner.

When I subsequently convinced Stephen to switch to radiology, his parents barred me from their home, saying now their son was no longer a real doctor. This subsequently changed of course as they realized what a good decision this had been. In later life they would want to send a car to pick me up for dinner, having saved their son from a life he certainly would not have enjoyed.

Anyhow, I called Stephen in Rhode Island. "How about coming back to Florida?" I asked. "We will be equal partners from day one, with two hospitals and an office." I guess it was a cold day, maybe some snow in Rhode Island, but Stephen said he would call back. It didn't take long. "I'm on my way," he said.

Sternberg and Schulman, PA was born, the best partnership I could have ever hoped for, certainly better than my second marriage. Lorraine and I went separate ways in late 1973.

Jim and Stephen   Happy Times   early 1990's

Chapter Sixteen – Equipment Time

Grant Bennett Community Hospital was moving along. Moselle and I organized a medical staff. Pending later elections, Fernandez would be the first Chief of Staff, I would be Vice-Chief and Stephen and I were Co-Chiefs of radiology, again with no contract. Why is this important? The American College of Radiology, the chief governing body of radiology always recommended having no contract.

The radiologist should be treated just like every other physician on staff, a member of the medical staff subject to the same rules and regulations. By Florida statute and in most states, a member of a medical staff cannot be removed from the staff without cause. On the contrary, if you are operating under a contract, the hospital can find other ways to terminate your privileges.

At almost every hospital, the administration is at odds with the radiologists. For every radiological procedure, there is a technical and a professional component. The technical component belongs to the hospital. They charge X number of dollars for their costs like equipment, personal, etc.

The radiologist charges for the professional component. This is for the interpretation of the examination and the supervision of the department. The technicians seem to be working for the radiologists, but are actually hospital employees and paid by the hospital.

When a radiologic examination is performed in a hospital, the hospital charges about two-thirds, the radiologist one-third. And the radiologist prefers to do his own billing. All hospital administrators see radiology and other hospital based physicians like anesthesia, pathology and the emergency room as a chance to increase their revenues. At the same time, the radiologist is trying to protect his domain. It's a constant never-ending battle, whether in the open or behind closed doors.

The administration hates the money hungry radiologist and the radiologist can never turn his back. But if the radiologist is operating without a contract, the administration loses some of their power. And no hospital wants the alternative, two groups of radiologists competing in the same hospital.

As Healthcare Corporation was building the hospital, they came to me and asked, "What brand of equipment should we go with?" They had contracts with most of the major companies and in those days, General Electric, Siemens, and Picker were the big ones. They were all good, the important factor was how good was their service department.

In our area, there was also a smaller brand name, Profexray. Their equipment was OK, perhaps not with all the bells and whistles, and a bit less expensive. If you wanted to put a x-ray machine to do just chest x-rays in your office, they were fine. The trouble was their service department or lack thereof.

So when Healthcare Corp asked me the question, I said, "Whoever you like, I don't care as long as it is not Profexray." You guessed it; they gave me an entire department of Profexray equipment. Stay tuned for the rest of that story.

Chapter Seventeen – Bennett Hospital Opens

OK, time for the big opening. The dedication ceremony was Sunday, December 8, 1974, with Wendall Cherry, David Jones, Herb Moselle, Alberto Fernandez, the first administrator Larry Bowdren, special guest Art Linkletter, and a couple of others from Louisville. We received some good press in the local papers and were open for business the next day.

Now Stephen and I had two hospitals and the office. We hired another radiologist, but it soon became evident that the office was counterproductive, requiring full time coverage. It was just as easy to have the out-patients come to the hospital. This came with a cost for in the hospital setting we lost the ability to completely control the flow of the out-patient work as before in our office.

No longer could we say that a 10:00 AM appointment guaranteed getting seen at 10:00. No longer could we meet each patient. We had lost this control to the staff employees who were working for the hospital. But the hospital flourished and our group grew larger.

It didn't take long for relations with Humana, as Extendicare was now called, to get testy. The Profexray equipment started breaking down the first day and their service department could not keep up with the repairs. As soon as they put a bandage somewhere, another one was needed. I'll spare you the details, but at the end of the first year of operation, Humana as the management company made the necessary decision to pull out all the radiological equipment from the department and replace it entirely with General Electric.

And of course, yup, you guessed it. They placed the entire blame on yours truly. They insisted It was all my idea to go with Profexray in the first place and now look what I had cost them. There were not going to be any more trips to the Kentucky Derby. From this point on, the relationships between radiology and administration only went from bad to worse.

But what could they do? They were stuck with us since we had no contract. They had to treat us like any other hospital staff member, and so we continued as radiologists basically 'in perpetuity.' Not wanting to be involved, I did not run for Vice-Chief of staff in the election of officers. We just wanted to do our thing.

Since I was Public Enemy Number One in the sight of the administration, Stephen and I decided I would work mostly at Margate and Stephen at Bennett. This would insure more continuity; we would be able to follow the patients on a more daily basis.

When the five year administrative contract was finished, Humana of course exercised their option to purchase the hospital for about five million dollars, a real bargain. All the investors in West Broward Investments, LLC made some money.

Humana promptly changed the name to Westside Regional Hospital. But they forgot to remove the plaque by the front door with my name on it, placed there when the hospital first opened. It was still there the last time I looked.

But the battle was not over. More fun was still to come.

DEDICATION ANNOUNCEMENT

Bennett Community Hospital opens in 1974 – Note the 'heavily' populated surroundings, nothing but empty spaces. We had opened in the middle of nowhere. Compare this to the next photo.

Now renamed Westside Regional Hospital - 1993
Compare this to the previous photo to see the community growth

Today, 2023, the corner of University Drive
and West Broward Boulevard is a very busy intersection,
with little space left for expansion

Chapter Eighteen – P O D C

Cravero had built a five story office building in front of Bennett hospital on a portion of the other ten acres. The area was growing significantly. West Broward Boulevard was now a paved four lane highway extending far west of the hospital and the long-awaited mall across the street was up and open. Shops and other office buildings had sprouted and many physicians had moved their offices further west. We were no longer 'west' but as I had anticipated, we were becoming the center of a thriving community. Max had his hospital on West Oakland Park and a bit further north, University Hospital had opened on University Drive.

It was time to become innovative and move forward. The concept of physician owned imaging centers was just beginning. With Stephen leading this idea in the early 1980's, we opened an imaging center in Cravero's office building with many of the local physicians who utilized imaging as limited partners.

It was named PODC, Physicians Out-Patient Diagnostic Center. Physicians who rarely requested (notice not 'ordered') radiology services were not offered shares in the venture. This was before the advent of CT or MRI, but PODC performed all other radiologic services. For this venture, we had little problem signing up limited partners, especially those who had missed out on our original hospital project.

Talk about throwing gasoline on a fire. Here we were, right in front of the hospital draining off as much of their out-patient work as possible. No more two-thirds/one-third. This was our new office and easy to cover. Of course, it became so busy we soon needed a full-time radiologist in the office.

The idea of physician owned imaging centers as compared to solely radiologist owned imaging centers was and still is a very controversial subject. The position of The American College of Radiology promotes the latter. But in the 1980's it was becoming a popular idea and we were certainly at the forefront.

In the meantime, in the early 1980's, the Margate medical community had grown significantly and was out-growing the original facility. Hospital Corporation of America rebuilt Margate General Hospital, moving the hospital from Margate Blvd to a completely newly constructed building on Route 441 in north Margate. They opened as Northwest Regional Medical Center.

But the first half of the 80's was only the calm before the storm. Trouble was brewing on the horizon.

Chapter Nineteen – CT & My Best Prediction

As noted, the first half of the 1980's was relatively smooth. We had our two hospitals and the imaging center. Our radiology group now numbered twelve, but Stephen and I were the only partners. The other ten radiologists were on salary, but everyone seemed happy.

When Stephen and I were in training as radiology residents, procedures were relatively simple. Besides the usual plain films, the gastrointestinal studies, barium enemas, IVP's (kidney studies), we did lots of angiography, some very basic nuclear medicine examinations, and a few other studies.

However, while in practice, new innovations in radiology seemed to come along every day. Nuclear medicine made rapid advances and ultrasound was now a diagnostic tool. We had to learn these new modalities on our own. For example, Stephen and I spent two weeks in San Francisco studying ultrasound at some fancy hospital.

Then I remember one day in Margate, before the hospital moved its location, the administrator came to me smiling (which in itself was unusual) and said, "We will be putting the van with the CT scanner in our parking lot tomorrow to start doing studies." Huh? What's CT I thought, smiling back and thinking, "What the hell is that?"

Well of course I knew what CT was. I had read a lot about it in our journals but to actually be doing it? And Westside was getting one too. Yup, off to CT school. But CT was pretty easy. It was just anatomy and in the early days, it was pretty straight forward, not too difficult. There were usually only sixteen images for each study.

Stephen and I hired Dr. Jerry Sheldon, a CT expert working at Mount Sinai Hospital in Miami Beach to come up once a week to review our cases and help with our self-training.

We stumbled along pretty well. I went to several CT weekend workshops.

At one of these, I overheard some radiologists talking about a new modality, something called magnetic resonance imaging or MRI, something with magnets instead of radiation.

I remember making my worse prognostic statement (this is why I was terrible in the stock market). I said, "Well, that's certainly something that will never happen in radiology."

Brilliant prediction, Jim.

Chapter Twenty – 2 MR Centers

Like my stock market predictions, I couldn't have been more wrong. MR was about to revolutionize radiology. And Stephen was brilliant. The partners in the PODC imaging center wanted to add MR but there was no space. MR centers need lots of space. They require extra shielding and in the early days, their computers were the size of a small house.

But in keeping with our previous experience, it was time to form another limited partnership and sign up some referring physicians. No problem, we were getting pretty good at doing this and had a good track record in what was now a thriving medical community.

Initially the only physicians utilizing magnetic resonance were orthopedic surgeons and neurologists/neurosurgeons. In the latter half of the 80's we bought a closed bank building on University Drive in Plantation. The cost of a top-notch scanner, a General Electric Signa 1.5 Tesla was about a million and a half dollars.

So no more shares for $700 like it was back in 1972. Shares now went for $20,000 with a limit of four to eligible physicians like orthopedists and neurologists. We had no trouble getting financing and were open for business, an LLC as usual. We hired a radiologist with MR fellowship training, set up the LLC so most of the profits went to the referring doctors and we took a piece, plus our reading fees.

Home run! MR was just getting started and the fees were high compared to now. $1800 plus extra sequence charges was the norm. The limited partners, who did nothing except send cases were making well over 100% return. One quarter, one partner had the nerve to call

Stephen complaining he had only made an 80% return on his investment that quarter.

Yes, the place was a gold mine but not because the partners were abusing it. MR was becoming the hottest imaging tool since Roentgen discovered the x-ray just before 1900. Word of course spread. A friend of one of our partners, an orthopedic surgeon in North Miami, called saying, "We want an MR center here too."

No problem, with a track record of what was happening in our Plantation MR office, it took no time to form another LLC and sell shares to a group of physicians in North Miami. All they had to do was call their friends at our first center and ask "Is this for real?" Now we had two centers and we thought we were done. We had no idea what we had started.

But let's get back to that later. In the meantime, things were not going well for us at Northwest Regional Hospital.

Chapter Twenty One – The Attempted Coup

I was spending almost all my time in Margate at NWMC, now known as Northwest Medical Center and owned by Hospital Corporation of America. I wish I could say something good about them, but I can't. If I thought the administrators at Westside were our antagonists, these guys up here made the Westside guys look like our best friends. But again, what could they do? We were doing a good job and the medical staff was happy with us so it was a stand-off. We had been there forever without a contract and intended to be there as long as we wanted.

Suddenly war was declared. But not from the administration directly. One of the radiologists in our group, Gerald Schmitt, along with three others, had organized a coup attempt to take over the radiology department and have us thrown out. Where did this come from? And of course the administrator, Joseph Feith, was thrilled with the idea. Why? Who knows what kind of a deal he had made with the renegades.

But Feith had a problem. Fortunately, we had no contract to cancel. And Florida state law required just cause and hearings by the medical staff to have a physician removed. Feith had nothing. Schmitt had persuaded a few of the medical staff to support his quartet but it was a tiny minority. A staff election was coming up so just to spite them, I ran for office for treasurer and won. Feith was furious; now he had to deal with me on the executive committee as an officer.

So Feith created his own nightmare, something no hospital administrator ever wants. He permitted two groups of radiologists to compete in the hospital at the same time. This meant that every time a physician requested (not ordered) an x-ray examination, the physician had to specify which group he wanted to read it. Sternberg or Schmitt?

Can you just imagine the chaos? First, none of the medical staff wanted to bother doing this. There were a lot of unspecified request forms. The radiology receptionist or technician had to call the referring physician. Or they could put the form in our stack or Schmitt's.

So we had to check every day since Schmitt took many of ours and changed the name of the radiologist from mine to his. Our group was doing 80-90 percent of the cases while Schmitt had a small group of referring physicians.

In the radiology department, I had a nice spacious office in which to work and read films. Also, there was a private bathroom. There was a large general reading room where other radiologists worked and where we reviewed cases with referring physicians. Feith had all my personal effects moved from my private office to the general room so Schmitt could have my nice office. There wasn't much I could do about that.

What I did resent was the loss of the private bathroom. No reason other than just general principles. But this was easy to solve. I acquired a large port-a-potty, put it in the center of the general reading room and encouraged everyone, both the radiologists and referring physicians to use it. It had no walls, it was just a big bowl.

My dentist friend Steven Margolin (the dentist mentioned earlier who accepted no lawyers as patients) named this Operation Toilet Bowl. It wasn't unusual for someone to come into the reading room and I or someone else was sitting there, taking a dump.

At first, Feith told housekeeping not to touch it. But how many days could this go on before the referring physicians started complaining? After all, they had to come into the room to review their cases and it was really getting putrid. This was a lot of fun for a few weeks. Feith finally had to get housekeeping to clean it on a daily basis.

So what was the final outcome of this fiasco? In early January of 1988, HCA banned our group from the hospital, saying it was a business decision, and therefore they had the right to do so. To hell with the hospital by-laws, no just cause, no hearings, just "You guys are out."

We immediately filed a lawsuit against HCA and were awarded a temporary injunction, returning us to work. HCA appealed this injunction in the 4th District court. A 2-1 decision re-barred us on January 8, 1988, pending further review by the lower courts, probably months away.

So we were out of Northwest Regional. And that was to be the end of my career working as a diagnostic radiologist. It was also the beginning of my career as a full-time businessman owning and operating MR centers.

It was strange. I had never looked upon radiology as 'work'. I loved what I was doing, problem solving, being a superspecialist. I had expected to be doing this forever. If you had told me I would only spend about twenty years reading films, I never would have thought it possible barring some physical impairment.

Marsha and Jim early 1990's

Chapter Twenty Two – I M I, Inc

Stephen and I now turned our full attention to our MR business. We realized we needed more manpower and made Ashley Kaye, one of our radiologists a full partner. Did you think we would stop with two centers? Little did we realize what we had started. Stephen saw it better than I did. He was a real visionary. We formed a new company, IMI, International Magnetic Imaging, Inc.

A third MR partnership and office on Glades Road in front of the Boca Raton hospital quickly followed and that became our main office of operation. I was now married to Marsha and we were to live in Boca Raton from 1989-1994.

Over the course of the next few years, from 1987 to 1994, using the same limited partnership formula, we opened and were operating MR centers in South Miami, Ft Lauderdale, Plantation, North Miami, and Boca Raton. In addition, we opened three centers in Chicago, IL and one each in Kansas City KS, Arlington Virginia, Indianapolis Indiana, San Juan Puerto Rico and Columbia South Carolina. We became the largest physician owned MR company at that time in the country.

Selling shares was so easy. We just had the prospective physician investor call one of our local partners to confirm. In the meantime I had more Frequent Flyer Miles on Delta and others than I could use. Stephen, Ashley, and I divided up covering the centers and kept calling on them to ensure everything was running smoothly. We hired MR fellowship trained radiologists to work in each center.

Of course, there had to be one that didn't turn out so well. We had made contact in Nassau, Bahamas with the most important physician group, which included the Minister of Health. But instead of our usual LLC arrangement, we were trying to make a deal with just these four doctors. With all the history of turmoil in the Bahamian government, maybe that was not such a good idea.

I should have started getting suspicious when our contact guy from Nassau took us to the local bank to open an account. I gave the bank president a check for $25,000 to open our account. When I later wrote a check for $10,000 it bounced. Strange, but upon inquiry, it seems the bank president had thought it was 'bribe' money for himself to help move the deal along.

The four-man doctor group had a large building, their lab, which they vacated for us to rent for the center. It was understood we would pay the rent we owed after we opened. As construction proceeded, we made multiple trips to Nassau meeting with everyone, the shielding was installed, and it was approaching time to deliver the magnet.

But I was starting to have second thoughts about this project. I wasn't sleeping well, thinking about this deal with no investor money up front. Why were we doing it this way? The night before the magnet was due for delivery in Nassau, I woke up in the middle of the night in a panic and called Stephen. "We can't do this," I said. "I don't trust any of these guys. The minute they get that magnet they will nationalize it."

We cancelled the magnet, sent it to another center, and never went back. The Bahamian group called complaining about the rent money, etc, but we were never available. I know our names were on a list at Bahamian Immigration if we ever were to try to go back. We just ate the losses. Stephen did go back to Nassau once twenty years later on vacation and said he had no problem. Me, forget it.

But hey, one strike-out wasn't so bad. The other centers were doing great, but unfortunately too great. We were about to suffer from our success. MR was in its infancy but growing leaps and bounds. The physicians were not ordering (sorry, Bernie) MR to put a dollar in their pocket. Today you can hardly get a plain x-ray. Everything is CT or MR. We just happened to be at the right place at the right time. And our centers were top-notch. The best possible equipment, large comfortable waiting and dressing rooms, good locations and parking, a fellowship trained radiologist on-site, no expense spared.

Meanwhile, a congressman from California, Pete Stark was actively pushing legislation to ban self-referral. After all, he knew that obviously the only reason those greedy doctors were sending patients for MR scans, or any procedures, was to put more money in their pockets.

And he personally was going to put a stop to this with federal legislation. If he could get Medicare and Medicaid to refuse payment, to make it actually illegal for a physician to refer a patient to a center where he had a financial interest, he could put a stop to this.

And without going into the long boring legislative details, he succeeded. The first Stark laws, Stark One, had banned referring to your own laboratory. But we were not a lab.

As the biggest physician owned MR company at the time, we were one of his prime targets. Someone leaked the financials of two of our Florida centers to the Palm Beach Post. We had a lot of angry partners when the Post wrote that "Dr. X made $120,000 last year on his $80,000 investment for sending his patients to........." They listed everyone. The Florida Medical Board was interested in talking to us, 60 Minutes called, newspersons were hiding in the bushes outside our Boca Raton office.

Everyone tried to think of ways to avoid the problem. You send to my center, I'll send to your center, put it in your wife's name, etc, etc, etc. Because if Medicare stopped paying, the private insurers would follow.

And there was talk of civil and criminal penalties. But none of these schemes were going to work. The only exception was if you were a publicly traded company. This was on the theory that your referrals wouldn't make much difference in such a big company.

All right, so let's go public. I called my friend Jimmy Cayne in New York, the CEO of Bear, Stearns. Would Bear, Stearns be interested in doing a public offering? Maybe; he sent some of his team to Boca Raton to take a look and talk. Unfortunately, this never got off the ground. Jimmy was mad at me for what he felt was a waste of his time, but he got over it. But that was just Jimmy Cayne being Jimmy.

A deadline was approaching as Stark II was about to go into effect which would bar payment at our centers for Medicare patients. Since these were a very significant percentage of our patients, we would be out of business. We found a publicly traded company, Consolidated, Inc that was interested in buying our centers.

But of course, they knew we were under pressure to sell so we were not going to be getting top dollar. At 11:59 PM, on September 30, 1994 in Consolidated lawyer's office in New York, we closed a deal just under the wire, selling the centers. IMI was gone.

Once the centers were owned by non-physicians, do you think the same 'spare no expense' policies were in place? Now it was the bottom line. Cut expenses, usually send the images for reading off-site, who knows where. Do you think the Stark II laws were better for the patients?

Remember the Gang of Four from Northwest Regional that tried to take over? One of them asked to and did come back to our group. Stephen, Ashley, and I sold our radiology interest at Westside Hospital to him and the other five radiologists in our group.

An exciting run had come to an end.

Vickie and Jim - 2019

Chapter Twenty Three – West Broward Today

'West' west Broward today? It's a far cry from the early 70's. The population figures tell the story. In 1970 Plantation had a population of 20,000. Today that figure is 95,000. Margate has gone from a 1970 figure of 8800 to 58,000 in the last census.

Aerial view of Plantation today, 2023
Compare to the views on pages 26 & 27 from the 1970's

An aerial view of Margate today, 2023
Compare to the aerial view on page 35 from 1970

Both Westside and Northwest Regional have expanded to more than twice their original size, adding both in and out-patient facilities. The towns of Plantation and Margate are heavily populated, roads expanded, innumerable businesses have opened. Physician offices are everywhere and there are several new free-standing diagnostic centers with CT and/or MR. The two other hospitals, Max's Florida Medical Center and University Hospital have also expanded.

I'm proud to have been a pioneer in moving medicine west, going where, as they say in space, 'no man had gone before', by building those two hospitals in the middle of nowhere. Would this have happened without me? Sure, as there was no other direction to go. Someone else would likely have 'gone west'. It was an opportunity that probably can't be repeated.

Right time, right place. I, radiologist did it.

Chapter Twenty Four – Epilogue

In hindsight, if I had to choose which part of my radiology career was the best, it's a no-brainer. The years I spent in solo practice in my little Plantation office would rate number one, two and three. It was one of the happiest times of my life. I was doing exactly what I had always dreamed of doing. I had no boss, I was on a friendly first name basis with all my referring doctors who I saw frequently and often socialized with. I met the patients. If a patient asked me too many questions, my stock answer was simple: "be sure to bring that up with your doctor when you see him to go over your results."

I probably was making less money per year than I would later but it's hard to compare the dollar value of 1970 with 1990. Then my career in the hospitals would rate second. Whoops, second and third are taken, so the hospital life ranked fourth. In those days, before the digital age, we had real hardcopy film. So every physician had to come to radiology to review their patient's films. We discussed the case and they often sought my opinion on how to proceed. I felt involved.

In the hospital I probably spent only 30-40% of my time actually sitting down and dictating reports. That was the easy part of the day. The rest of the day I was doing procedures, talking with the doctors, often working with my technicians on various aspects of their work, lunching in the doctors' lunch room to talk to everyone, etc. I kept track of my cases and knew the follow-up.

A radiologist has to have at least a working knowledge of the technical aspects of taking films. Imagine a race car driver who had no idea what was under the hood of the car or a pilot with no idea why his aircraft flew, only knowing how to fly it.

If a technician brought me a study and wanted to know if it needed repeating for better quality, I usually said yes, repeat it without even looking at it. After all, if the technician wasn't happy with a film, how did he think I was going to feel? But it wasn't enough to just say, "Repeat it." A good radiologist could talk their technical language and explain what to do. I was a pretty good technician and had their respect.

For the most part, the residents coming out of residency today have had no technical training; they wouldn't know how take a chest x-ray. I always encouraged them to try to spend at least a little time during residency with the technicians. At least learn a few of the basics. You never know where you are going to end up.

In Margate Hospital, I think I kept every technician for all the years I was there. Any turnover in the private office had usually been the technician getting married and leaving, or getting pregnant. In those years, most radiologists were a happy bunch. So what has changed? Why now is burnout such a major problem for radiologists?

In my opinion, the worst thing that has happened to the radiologist was the arrival of the digital age and the PACS (Picture Archiving Communication Systems) reading equipment in the hospitals. I became familiar with this when I started teaching in the summers.

Today the diagnostic radiologist sits in a secluded cubby hole or small room and spends 99% of his working hours reading and dictating films into a machine. And reading CT or MR images are a nightmare. There are just too many images to read. They just keep scrolling back and forth on the same case. Often I would look at one of these cases with a resident. When I would come back 15-20 minutes later, they were still scrolling the same case.

But I also think a major factor is that the PACS system permits the referring physician to look at the films on the hospital floor. Who needs the radiologist? After all, many of the referring physicians were specialists who felt they could do their own interpretation.

In the fifteen or so summers I spent teaching up north, I can count on one hand the total number of times a referring physician actually came to the radiology department.

There wasn't a single radiology resident who would know the referring physician even if he had a name tag. Very sad, I'd be burned out too. All the enjoyment is gone. There is no follow-up on the cases you report, no interaction, nothing but sit in your cage and crank 'em out. The diagnostic radiologist feels uninvolved in the cases.

No wonder diagnostic radiology ranks high for burn-out in the medical specialties. Think about their attitudes now compared to how I felt about it. I think it's really a shame. I couldn't wait to go in each morning. Now the average radiologist can't wait to get out. Maybe progress is not always progress.

So now what? Part of the deal with Consolidated was that Stephen, Ashley, and I would receive significant compensation for three years as part of a non-compete agreement. Great – I certainly had no interest in competing anyhow so this was a big bonus.

At Northwest Regional Hospital, the Gang of Four, (now three) didn't last a year. The hospital replaced them with a group from out-of-town. At Westside Hospital, our former associates, inexperienced at being in charge, could not provide the services the hospital required. Having never been in a decision-making position, they were replaced within two years.

I was married to Marsha and we were looking forward to new chapters. I discovered I was a good teacher. From 1994 – 1999, we spent three months each spring in Rome, Italy. I learned to speak Italian and was teaching radiology in a hospital associated with the university.

We spent the summers in western North Carolina during those years and then moved to Minneapolis, her hometown. I was appointed assistant professor of radiology at the University of Minnesota where I continued my teaching career for two years.

After Marsha's sudden, unexpected passing in 2001, I bought an apartment in Chicago and had the same position at Rush University during the summers for eleven years.

In 2008, I met Vickie Bader and we have been together ever since. After Chicago, Vickie and I rented an apartment in Milwaukee where I continued teaching for four years until the pandemic. The past fifteen winters I have spent my time playing and teaching bridge.

The pandemic gave me a lot of free time and I published seventeen books on various topics on the game of bridge. Now Vickie and I travel abroad a lot in the summer. We usually go to Italy where we have many friends, mostly radiologists from my days teaching there in the 90's. Good friends, great food, drink the Italian reds. What could be better?

Tomorrow? Who knows?

Printed in the United States
by Baker & Taylor Publisher Services